THE TREEHOUSE JOKE BOOK

ANDY GRiFFiTHS
illustrated by
TERRY DENTON

Feiwel and Friends • New York

A FEIWEL AND FRIENDS BOOK
An imprint of Macmillan Publishing Group, LLC
120 Broadway, New York, NY 10271

Our books may be purchased in bulk for promotional, educational, or
business use. Please contact your local bookseller or the Macmillan Corporate
and Premium Sales Department at (800) 221-7945 ext. 5442 or by email at
MacmillanSpecialMarkets@macmillan.com.

Library of Congress Cataloging-in-Publication Data is available.
ISBN 978-1-250-25950-9 (paperback) / ISBN 978-1-250-25949-3 (ebook)
Book design by Eileen Gilshian

Feiwel and Friends logo designed by Filomena Tuosto

Originally published in Australia by Pan Macmillan Australia Pty Ltd.
First published in the United States by Feiwel and Friends, an imprint of
Macmillan Publishing Group, LLC
First U.S. edition, 2020

10 9 8 7 6 5 4 3 2 1

mackids.com

CONTENTS

Q: What sort of stories do bears like best?

A: Furry tales.

Q: What do you call an angry bear?

A: Nothing—just run.

Q: What do bears do when it rains?

A: They get wet.

Q: What do Alexander the Great and Winnie the Pooh have in common?

A: They have the same middle name.

Q: **What's green, sticky, and smells like eucalyptus?**

A: Koala vomit.

Q: Why did Tigger go to the bathroom?

A: He was looking for his friend Pooh.

Q: Why do birds fly south in winter?

A: Because it's too far to walk.

Q: What do you call a seagull when it flies over the bay?

A: A bagel.

Q: What do you get if you cross a centipede with a parrot?

A: A walkie-talkie.

Q: What do you get if you cross a parrot with a shark?

A: A bird that will talk your ear off.

Don't shout!

Q: What is the most uncomfortable of all birds?

A: A wedgie-tailed eagle.

Q: Which bird is always out of breath?

A: A puffin.

Q: What is a bird's favorite part of the news?

A: The feather forecast.

Q: Why is a raven like a writing desk?

A: Because neither is made of cheese.

Q: What did the bird say at the sale?

A: Cheap! Cheap!

Q: What do you call a cockatoo
on an electric wire?

A: A shockatoo.

Q: What is orange and sounds like a parrot?

A: A carrot.

Q: What do you call birds that are in love?

A: Tweethearts.

Q: What do you give a sick bird?

A: Tweetment.

Q: Why did the baby bird get in trouble at school?

A: Because it was caught peeping at another bird's test.

Q: Why did the owl say "Tweet tweet"?

A: Because it couldn't give a hoot.

Q: Why did the bird bring toilet paper to the party?

A: Because it was a party pooper.

29

Q: What has garbage and flies?

A: A garbage truck.

Q: How do you talk to a giant?

A: Use big words.

Q: What cup can you never drink out of?

A: A hiccup.

Q: What demands an answer but asks no question?

A: A telephone.

Q: If a rooster laid a brown egg and a white egg, what kind of chicks would hatch?

A: None; roosters can't lay eggs.

Q: What has to be broken before you can use it?

A: An egg.

Q: What is pink and can think?

A: A brain.

Q: What is harder to catch the faster you run?

A: Your breath.

Q: What is the best way to win a race?

A: Run faster than everyone else.

Q: What is red and smells like blue paint?

A: Red paint.

Q: Why did the scientist put a knocker on her door?

A: Because she wanted the No-bell Prize.

Q: What is a tornado's favorite game to play?

A: Twister.

Q: What did zero say to eight?

A: "Nice belt!"

Q: Imagine you are
in a room with no doors
or windows or anything.
How do you get out?

A: Stop imagining!

Q: What gives you the ability to walk through walls?

A: Doors.

Q: What kind of room has no windows or doors?

A: A mushroom.

Q: What sort of table is always in the kitchen?

A: A vegetable.

CATNARY ISLANDS ©

Dear Jill,
Having a nice time. So far
we've been fishing, bird-
watching, bird-catching,
bird-eating, and
parasailing.
Lots of love,
Silky and the gang

To Jill
Jill's house
Near the forest
World

Q: **What can travel around the world while staying in a corner?**

A: A stamp.

Q: What do you call an old snowman?

A: Water.

Q: How do you put a giraffe into a refrigerator?

A: Open the refrigerator, put in the giraffe, and close the door.

Q: How do you put an elephant into a refrigerator?

A: Open the refrigerator, take out the giraffe, put in the elephant, and close the door.

Q: The lion king is hosting an animal meeting. All the animals attend, except one. Which animal does not attend?

A: The elephant. It is in the refrigerator.

Q: There is a river you must cross, but crocodiles live in it and you don't have a boat. How do you get across?

A: You swim across. Have you not been listening? All the crocodiles are at the lion king's meeting.

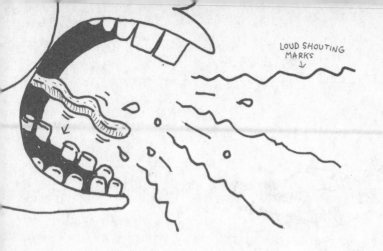

LOUD SHOUTING MARKS
↓

Q: **What breaks every time you name it?**

A: Silence.

CLOMP!

Q: What was the tallest mountain in the world before Mount Everest was discovered?

A: Mount Everest.

Q: What is the laziest mountain in the world?

A: Mount Ever-rest.

Q: Who can jump higher than the highest mountain?

A: Anybody can . . . because mountains can't jump!

Q: Why was six afraid of seven?

A: Because seven eight nine.

Q: What walks on four legs at the start of its life, two in the middle of its life, and three at the end?

A: A human.

Q: How do you get a mouse to smile?

A: Say "cheese."

Q: How do you spell candy with two letters?

A: C and Y.

Q: What is a gip?

A: A backward pig!

Q: What is a pig?

A: A backward gip!

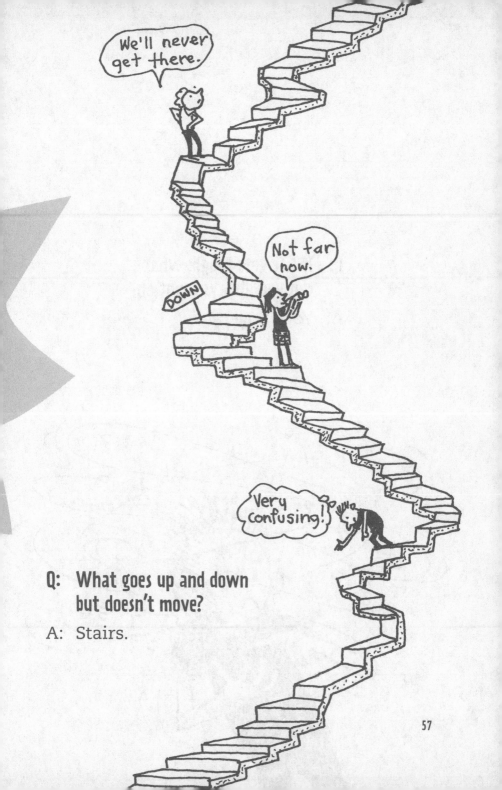

Q: What goes up and down but doesn't move?

A: Stairs.

Q: **If life gets tough, what can you always count on?**

A: Your fingers.

Q: When is a door not a door?

A: When it's ajar.

Q: What happens when you put a tooth into a glass of water?

A: It gets wet.

Q: What is good for a bald head?

A: Some hair.

Q: What did one eye say to the other eye?

A: There's something between us that smells.

Q: Why are robots never scared?

A: Because they have nerves of steel.

Q: How can you say rabbit
without using the letter R?

A: Bunny.

Q: There is a one-story house where everything is red. The roof is red, the floors are red, the walls are red, the carpet is red, the ceiling is red, the doors are red, all the furniture is red, and even the toilet is red. What color are the stairs?

A: There are no stairs because it's a one-story house!

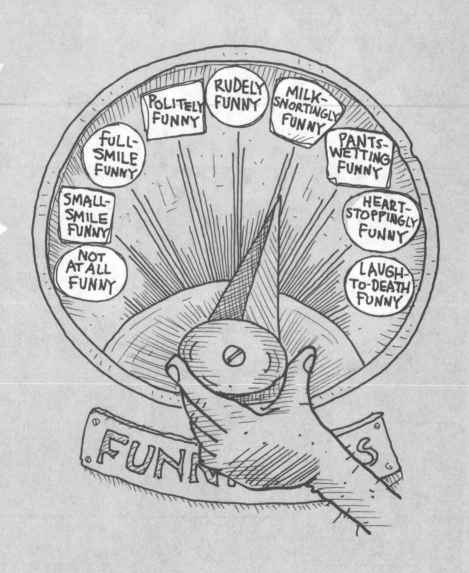

Q: How does a cat fly?

A: With a catapult.

CAT

Q: What do you get if you cross a lemon and a cat?

A: A sour puss.

Q: Why couldn't the cat drink its milk?

A: Because it didn't have a face.

Q: What did the disbelieving cat say?

A: "You've got to be kitten me!"

Q: What did the dog say to the little child pulling its tail?

A: "This is the end of me."

Q: What do cats have that nobody else does?

A: Baby cats.

Q: **What do you call a dog that can do magic tricks?**

A: A labracadabrador.

Q: **What is the goal of every adventurous cat?**

A: To climb every meow-ntain!

Q: What do you call a pile of cats?

A: A purr-amid.

Q: What does a polite cat always say?

A: "Paw-lease" and "thank you."

CHICKEN JOKES

Q: Why did the chicken cross the road?

A: To get to the other side.

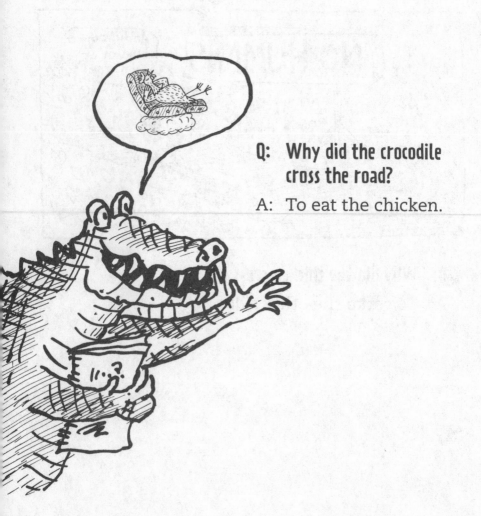

Q: Why did the crocodile cross the road?

A: To eat the chicken.

Q: How do chickens wake up in the morning?

A: With an alarm cluck.

Q: Why do hens lay eggs?

A: Because if they dropped them, they would break.

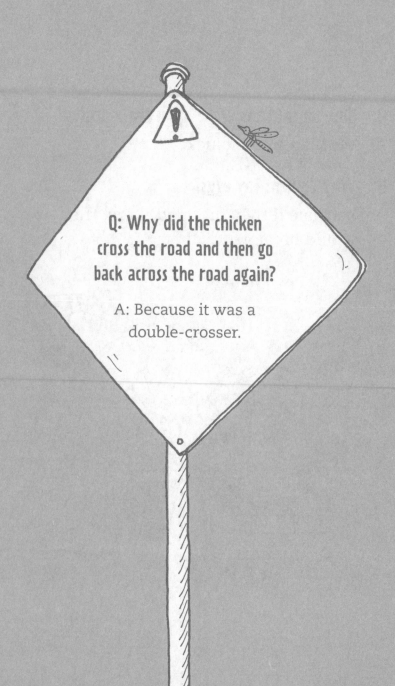

Q: Why did the chicken cross the road and then go back across the road again?

A: Because it was a double-crosser.

Q: Why did the chicken cross the road, roll in mud, and then go back across the road again?

A: Because it was a dirty double-crosser.

Q: Why did the chicken
cross the road?

A: I don't know.

To get to the shops.
Did you find that funny?

No.

Well, neither did the chicken
because the shops were closed.

Q: Why did the chicken take two book-character costumes to school?

A: Because it was "buk buk" week.

Q: Why did the turkey cross the road?

A: To prove it wasn't chicken.

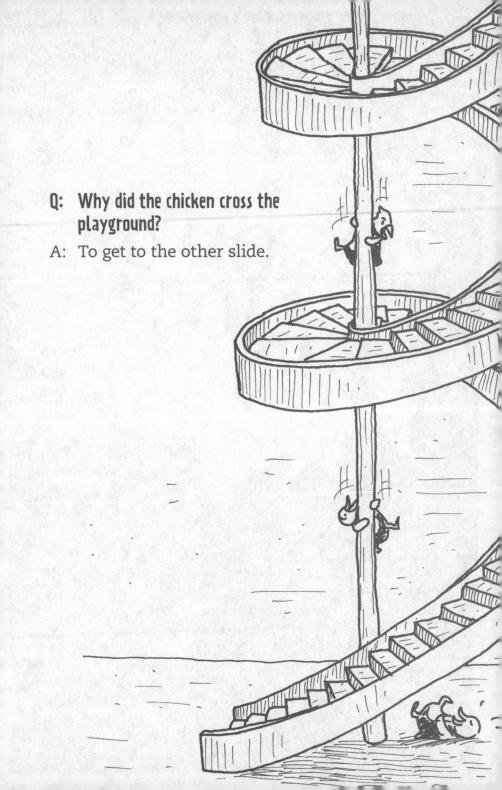

Q: Why did the chicken cross the playground?

A: To get to the other slide.

Q: Where do cows go when their TV is not working?

A: The moo-vies.

Q: When do cows not do their chores?

A: When they're not in the moood.

Q: What do you get if you walk under a cow?

A: A pat on the head.

Q: What do cows give after an earthquake?

A: Milkshakes.

Q: What do you call a cow that eats your grass?

A: A lawn mooer.

Q: What do you call a cow's bedtime stories?

A: Dairy tales.

DINOSAUR
JOKES

Q: What do you call a blind dinosaur?

A: An I-don't-think-it-saw-us.

Q: What do you call a sleeping dinosaur?

A: A dino-snore.

Q: Why did the dinosaur cross the road?

A: Because chickens hadn't evolved yet.

Q: What game do dinosaurs like to play with humans?

A: Squash.

Q: Why didn't the dinosaur cross the road?

A: Because roads hadn't been invented yet.

Q: Why can't you hear a
pterodactyl go to the bathroom?

A: Because it has a silent P.

Q: What do you get when you cross a dinosaur with fireworks?

A: Dino-mite!

ELEPHANT JOKES

Q: How can you tell if there is an elephant in your refrigerator?

So cool!

A: The door won't shut.

Q: How can you tell if an elephant has been in your refrigerator?

A: There are elephant footprints in the butter.

Q: Why are elephants wrinkly?

A: Because they don't fit on ironing boards.

Q: Why did the elephant stand on the marshmallow?

A: Because it didn't want to fall into the hot chocolate.

Q: What did the grape say when
the elephant stepped on it?

A: Nothing. It just gave out
a little whine.

Roll up, roll up...
Try your luck with
the TRUNKINATOR!

crab legs

Q: What is big and gray and flies straight up?

A: An elecopter.

Q: What's gray and powdery?

A: Instant elephant mix.

Q: Why do you never see elephants chewing gum?

A: Because they don't do it in public.

Q: Where do fish go on vacation?

A: Finland.

Q: Why do some fish live at the bottom of the ocean?

A: Because they dropped out of school.

Q: Which part of a mermaid weighs the most?

A: Her scales.

Q: How did the hammerhead shark do on her test?

A: She nailed it.

Q: Why do fish like to eat worms?

A: Because they get hooked on them.

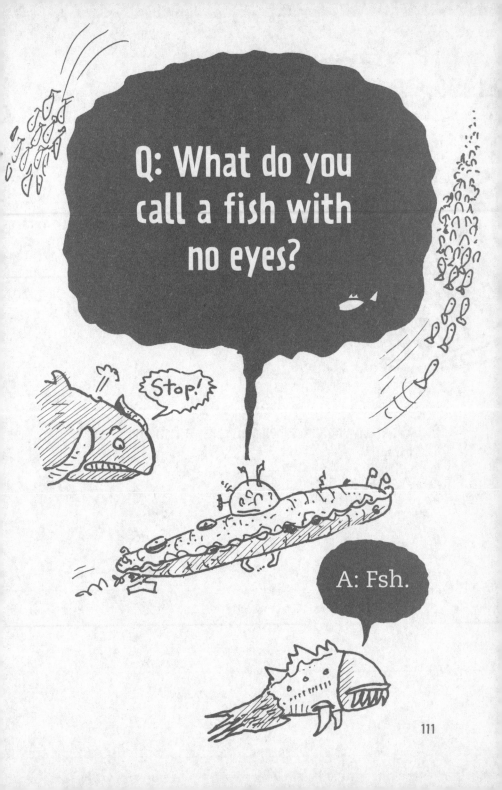

Q: What do you get when you cross a fish and a kitten?

A: A purr-anha.

Q: Why aren't crabs good at sharing?

A: Because they are shellfish.

Q: Who do clams call when they are hurt?

A: The clam-bulance.

Q: How do shellfish get around in the ocean?

A: Taxi-crabs.

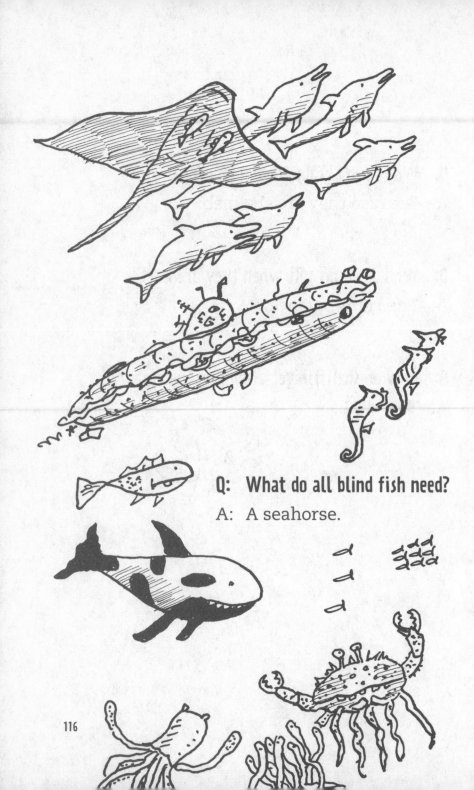

Q: What do all blind fish need?

A: A seahorse.

Q: How do you make an octopus laugh?

A: With ten-tickles.

**Q: What does a shark eat
with peanut butter?**

A: Jellyfish.

Q: Where do frogs keep their money?

A: In a riverbank.

Q: What's a frog's favorite year?

A: A leap year.

Q: What's a frog's favorite drink?

A: Croak-a-Cola.

Q: **What did the toad say to his sweetheart?**

A: "I toadly love you."

Q: **What happens when a frog's car breaks down?**

A: It gets toad.

Q: What wobbles and flies?

A: A jelly-copter.

Q: What's red and moves up and down?

A: A tomato in an elevator.

Q: Why did the tomato blush?

A: Because it saw the salad dressing.

Q: Why do bananas come in bunches?

A: So they're not lonely.

Q: What did the skeleton order for dinner?

A: Spare ribs.

Q: What's the difference between broccoli and snot?

A: Kids don't like to eat broccoli.

Q: What did the baby corn say to the mommy corn?

A: "Where's popcorn?"

Q: If I had six oranges in one hand and seven apples in the other, what would I have?

A: Big hands!

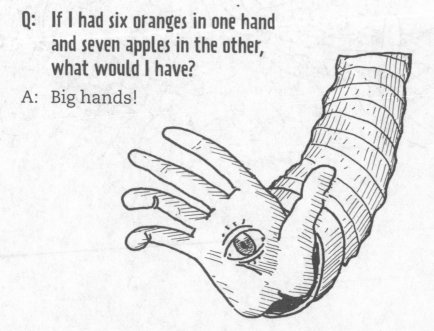

Q: Did you hear about the race between the lettuce and the tomato?

A: The lettuce was ahead and the tomato was trying to ketchup.

Q: How did the butcher introduce his wife?

A: "Meat Patty."

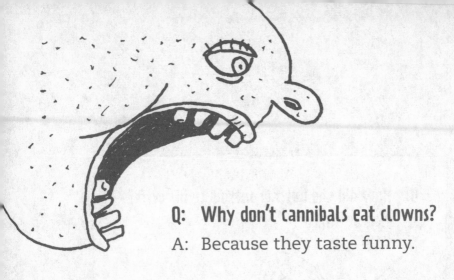

Q: Why don't cannibals eat clowns?

A: Because they taste funny.

Q: What does bread do on vacation?

A: Loaf around.

Q: What did the cheese say when it looked in the mirror?

A: "I look gouda."

Q: Why did the biscuit go to the doctor?

A: Because it was feeling crummy.

Q: What cake do you eat in a haunted house?

A: An i-scream cake.

Q: **What vegetables do librarians like?**

A: Quiet peas.

Q: What is the best thing to put into a pie?

A: Your teeth.

Q: **What is a monkey's favorite type of cookie?**

A: Chocolate chimp.

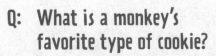

* * * * * * * *
* * * * * * * *
* * * * * * *
* * * * * * *
* * * * * * *
* * * * * * *
* * * * * * *
* * * * * * *
*

Q: What do snowmen eat for breakfast?

A: Snowflakes.

Q: **What do you call shoes made out of banana skins?**

A: Slippers.

Q: **Why did the banana go to see the doctor?**

A: Because it wasn't peeling well.

Knock knock.

Who's there?

Boo.

Boo who?

No need to cry about it.

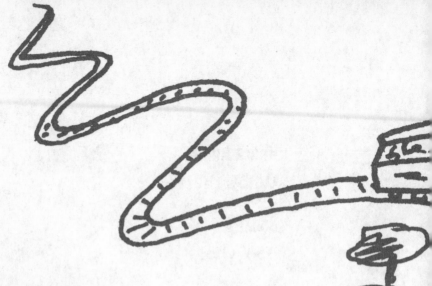

Knock knock.
Who's there?

Knock knock.
Who's there?

Knock knock.
Who's there?

Knock knock.
Who's there?

Aunt.
Aunt who?

Aunt you glad that I stopped?

142

Knock knock.
Who's there?

Chooch.
Chooch who?

Watch out for the train!

Knock knock.
Who's there?

Banana.
Banana who?

Knock knock.
Who's there?

Banana.
Banana who?

Knock knock.
Who's there?

Orange.
Orange who?

Wow, my picture is so good, it even tastes like a banana.

Orange you glad I didn't say banana?

Knock knock.

Who's there?

The interrupting volcano.

The interrupting volcano who?

Volcanoes don't interrupt. They erupt!

Knock knock.
Who's there?

Oscar.
Oscar who?

Oscar silly question, you get a silly answer.

Knock knock.

Who's there?

A little old lady.

A little old lady who?

I didn't know you could yodel.

Knock knock.

Who's there?

Interrupting cow.

Interrupting cow—

Moo!

Knock knock.
Who's there?

Cows.
Cows who?

Cows go moo, not who!

Knock knock.
Who's there?

Luke!
Luke who?

Luke through the keyhole and you'll see.

Knock knock.
Who's there?

Wooden shoe.
Wooden shoe who?

Wooden shoe like to know!

There's a call for Andy. It's his hairdresser.
LOOK WHO'S TALKING
He's wandered off somewhere with Terry. Tell her he'll call back.

Q: What did sushi A say to sushi B?

A: "Wassup, B?"

That reminds me... I must buy some more fish!

Q: What did one toilet say to the other toilet?

A: "You look flushed."

Q: What did the egg say to the clown?

A: "You really crack me up."

Q: Two sausages are in a frying pan. One says, "Is it just me or is it really hot in here?" What does the other one say?

A: "Wow! A talking sausage!"

Q: What did one pencil say to the other pencil?

A: "You're looking sharp!"

Q: What did the pen say to the pencil?

A: "So what's your point?"

Q: What did the teacher say when it rained cats and dogs?

A: "Be careful not to step in a poodle."

Q: What do sharks say when something amazing happens?

A: "Jaw-some!"

Q: **What did the earwig say as it fell off the cliff?**

A: "Ear we go!"

Q: What did one math book say to the other math book?

A: "Do you want to hear my problems?"

Q: **What did the bee say to the flower?**

A: "Hello, honey!"

Q: What did the balloon say to the pin?

A: "Hi, Buster!"

Q: What did one hat say to the other hat?

A: "You wait here. I'll go on ahead."

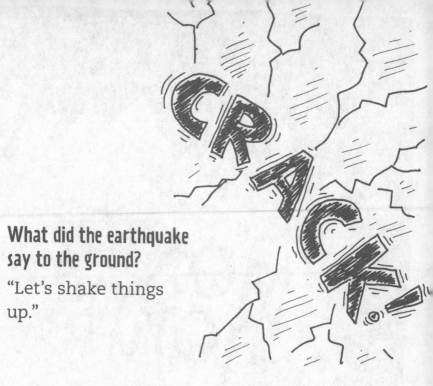

Q: What did the earthquake say to the ground?

A: "Let's shake things up."

Q: What did the judge say when the skunk walked into the courtroom?

A: "Odor in the court!"

Q: Is an old 100-dollar bill worth more than a new one?

A: Yes—it's worth 99 more dollars.

6... 7..8...9...10...11...12...13...14...
...19...20...21...22...23...24...
41... 65... 130... 260...
1040... 3072½...
... ...
220,604...
506,321...
999,996...

Q: What is the easiest way to double your money?

A: Put it in front of a mirror.

Q: If money really did grow on trees, what would be everybody's favorite season?

A: Fall.

Q: **What has 100 heads and 100 tails?**

A: 100 coins.

Q: **Where can you find money whenever you look for it?**

A: A dictionary.

 I wish I had enough
money to buy a dinosaur.

What would you
do with a dinosaur?

 Who wants a dinosaur?
I just want the money!

Q: If there are four dollars and you take away three, how many do you have?

A: You have three (that's what you took).

Q: What has a head and a tail but no body?

A: A coin.

Q: Why did the robber take a bath?

A: He wanted to make a clean getaway.

Q: What's a good way to save money?

A: Forget who you borrowed it from.

Q: How do monkeys make toast?

A: They put it on a gorilla.

Q: What type of key opens a banana?

A: A monkey.

Q: What's yellow and smells like bananas?

A: Monkey vomit.

Q: What was Andy and Terry's least favorite part of working at the zoo?

A: Filling in for the monkeys while the monkeys were on a break.

Q: How do you catch a monkey?

A: Climb a tree and act like a banana.

Q: What do you call a monkey that's really good at sports?

A: A chimp-ion!

Q: What do monkeys wear when they are cooking?

A: Ape-rons.

Q: What rocks but does not roll?

A: A rocking chair.

Q: What's a plumber's favorite song?

A: "Singin' in the drain."

Q: What kind of musical instrument do rats play?

A: Mouse organs.

Q: What is a mummy's favorite type of music?

A: Rap.

Q: How do you clean a dirty tuba?

A: With a tuba toothpaste.

Q: What game do cats like to play at birthday parties?

A: Mew-sical chairs.

Q: What's the best present you can receive for Christmas?

A: A broken drum—you just can't beat it!

A: A penguin.

Q: What do penguins sing at a birthday party?

A: "Freeze a jolly good fellow."

Q: What do penguins wear on their heads?

A: Ice caps.

PIRATE JOKES

Q: Why couldn't the pirate play cards?

A: Because he was sitting on the deck.

Q: How do pirates talk to one another?

A: Aye to aye.

Q: What is a pirate's favorite letter?

Arrrr.

Q: Where do pirates go to the bathroom?

A: On the poop deck.

Q: How much does it cost a pirate to get their ears pierced?

A: A buck-an-ear.

SCHOOL JOKES

AN ANDY AND TERRY LEARN-TO-READ BOOK

Q: What is the difference between a teacher and a train?

A: A teacher says, "Spit out your gum," and a train says, "Choo choo."

Q: Why did the teacher wear sunglasses to class?

A: Because her students were so bright.

Q: Where do belly buttons go to school?

A: The navel academy.

Q: Why did the elf go to school?

A: To learn the elf-abet.

Q: Why did the girl bring a ladder to school?

A: Because she wanted to get to high school.

Q: What is an owl's favorite subject?

A: Owl-gebra.

Q: What is a witch's favorite subject?

A: Spelling.

Q: What is a snake's favorite subject?

A: Hiss-tory.

Q: Why are tooth fairies so smart?

A: They gather a lot of wisdom teeth.

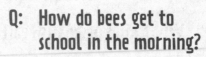

Q: How do bees get to school in the morning?

A: On the school buzz.

Q: What kind of ant is really good at math?

A: An accountant.

Q: Why was school easier for cave people?

A: Because there was no history class.

Q: What gives you information and is supersmooth?

A: A non-friction book.

Q: What building has the most stories?

A: A library.

Q: What has words but never speaks?

A: A book.

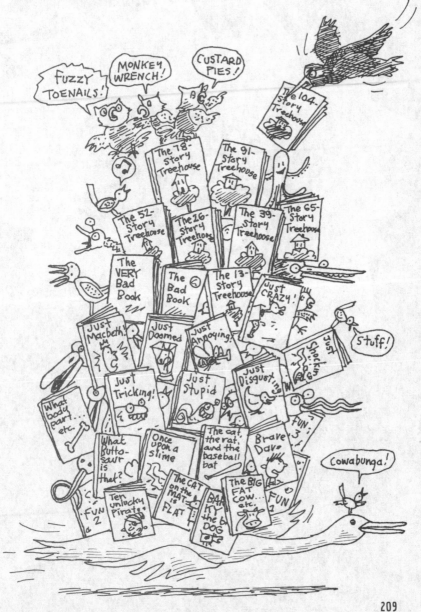

Q: What do you call a sheep without legs?

A: A cloud.

Q: Why did the sheep cross the road?

A: To get to the baa-ber.

Q: What do you call a sheep crossed with a kangaroo?

A: A woolly jumper.

Q: Why don't skeletons fight each other?

A: They don't have the guts.

Q: Why are ghosts such bad liars?

A: Because you can see right through them.

Q: Why didn't the skeleton go to the dance?

A: Because it didn't have anybody to go with.

Q: **What is a ghost's favorite game?**

A: Hide-and-screech.

Q: What's a zombie's least favorite room?

A: The living room.

Q: Where do zombies like to swim?

A: The Dead Sea.

BILL,
THE
ZOMBIE
POSTMAN

Q: What movie do monsters like?

A: *Scare Wars.*

Q: Where does Dracula keep his money?

A: In a blood bank.

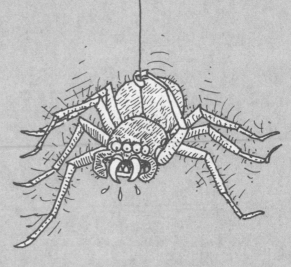

Q: Why couldn't Dracula's wife go to sleep?

A: Because of his coffin.

Q: Why does Dracula clean his
teeth three times a day?

A: To prevent bat breath.

Q: What did the werewolf eat after he
had his tooth fixed?

A: The dentist.

Q: What is Dracula's favorite fruit?

A: Neck-tarines.

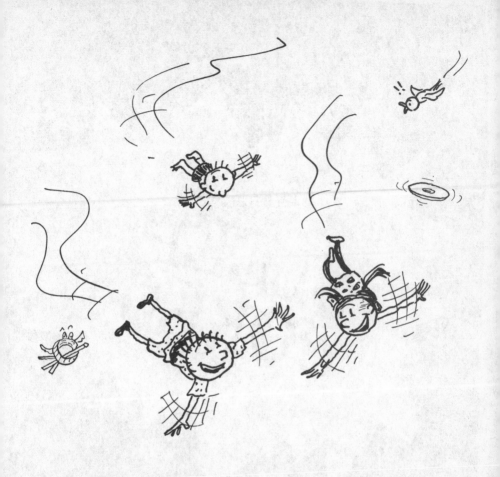

Q: Why do witches fly on brooms?

A: Because vacuum cleaners can't fly.

Q: What did the sheet say to the mattress?

A: "I've got you covered."

Q: Where does a spy sleep?

A: Undercover.

Q: **What's the last thing you take off before bed?**

A: Your feet—off the floor.

Q: Where do butterflies sleep?

A: On cater-pillows.

Q: What question can you never truthfully answer yes to?

A: "Are you asleep?"

Q: What do scuba divers wear to bed?

A: Snorkels.

Q: What do you call a sleepy bull?

A: A bulldozer.

Q: Did you hear about the soldier who bought a camouflage sleeping bag?

A: She can't find it.

Q: What boy wizard magically grew a beard each night as he slept?

A: Hairy Potter.

Q: Why are tall people the laziest?

A: Because they lie longer in bed.

Q: Where do books sleep?

A: Between their covers.

Q: Why does a dragon sleep all day?

A: So it can hunt knights.

Q: Why did the girl tiptoe past the medicine cabinet?

A: She didn't want to wake the sleeping pills.

Q: Where do astronauts leave their rockets?

A: At parking meteors.

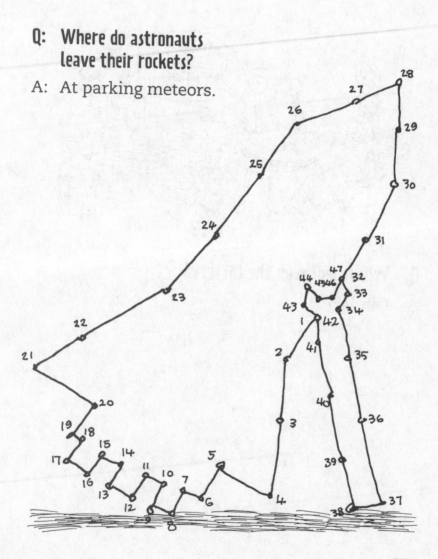

Q: Which Jedi won the lottery?

A: Obi-Won.

Q: What is Yoda's favorite car?

A: A Toyoda.

Q: What is fast, loud, and crunchy?

A: A rocket chip.

Q: What time do astronauts eat?

A: At launch time.

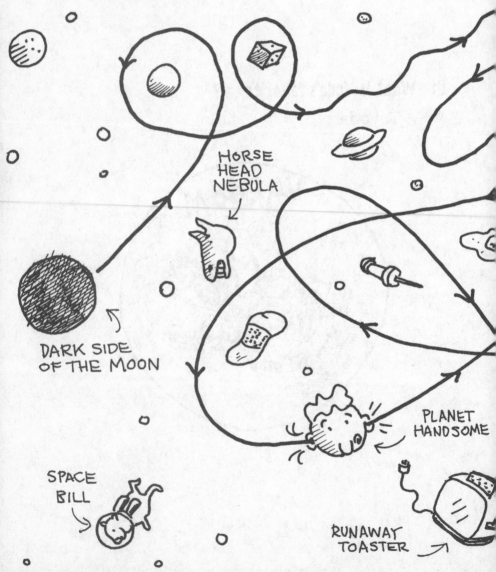

HORSE
HEAD
NEBULA

DARK SIDE
OF THE MOON

PLANET
HANDSOME

SPACE
BILL

RUNAWAY
TOASTER

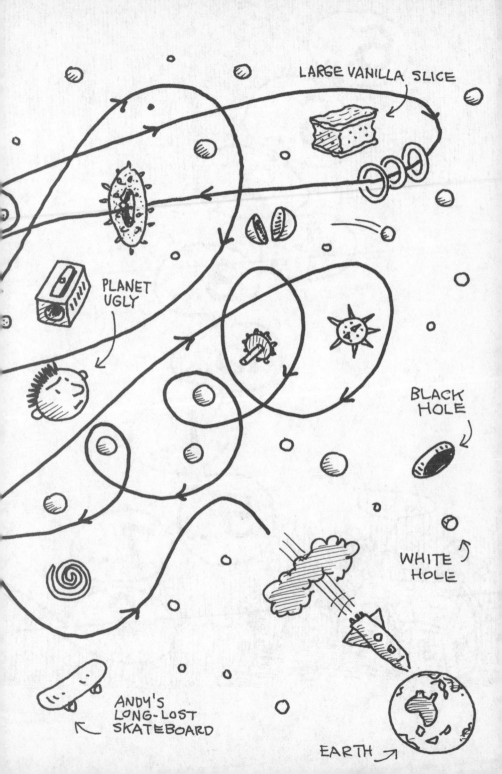

Q: What did the astronaut say to the rocket?
A: "You're fired."

Q: How do you get a baby astronaut to sleep?
A: You rocket.

you fools!

Q: How does the man in the moon cut his hair?

A: Eclipse it.

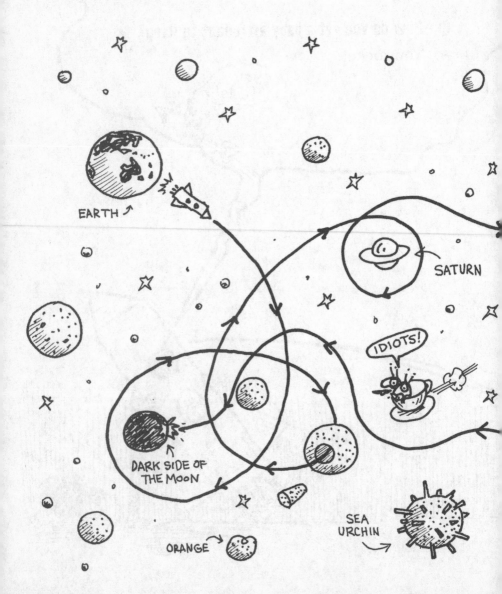

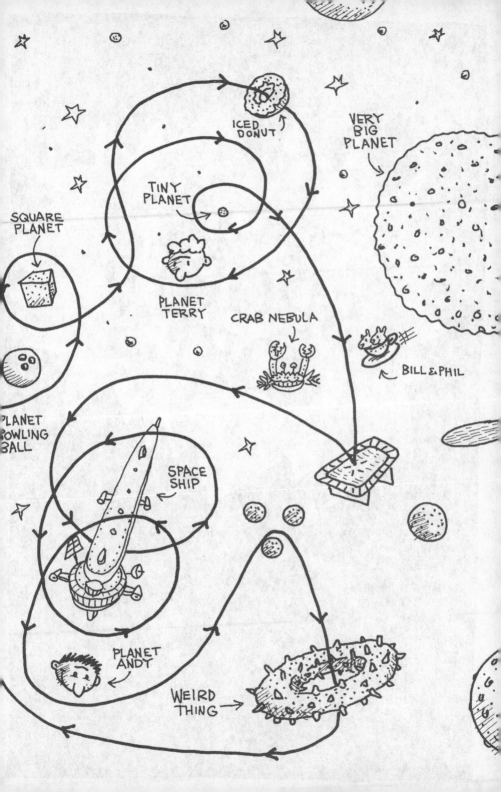

Q: What lights up a soccer stadium?

A: A soccer match.

Q: In what sport do winners go backward and losers go forward?

A: Tug-of-war.

Q: Why are artists no good in sports matches?

A: Because they keep drawing.

Q: Why did the golfer wear two pairs of pants?

A: In case he got a hole in one.

Q: Why was Cinderella kicked
off the soccer team?

A: Because she kept running away
from the ball.

Q: Why can't you play games in the jungle?

A: Because there will always be a cheetah.

← cheetah

Q: What position does a ghost play in soccer?

A: Ghoulie.

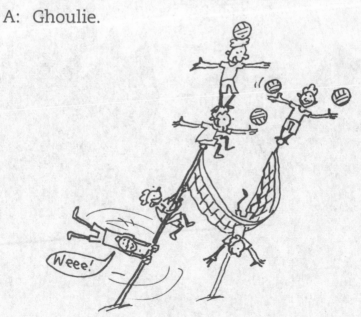

Weee!

Q: Why did the boy fall off his bike?

A: Because his mother threw
a refrigerator at him.

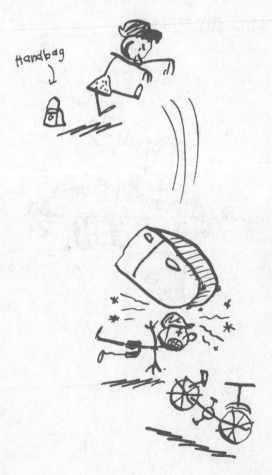

Handbag

Q: What did the farmer say when he couldn't find his tractor?

A: "Where's my tractor?"

Q: What did the farmer say
when he found his tractor?

A: "There's my tractor!"

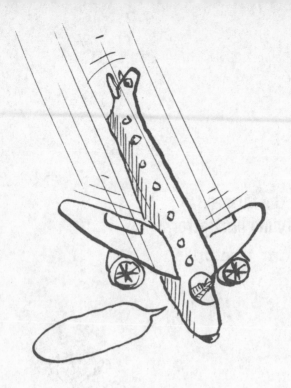

Q: Why did the plane crash?

A: Because the pilot was a loaf of bread.

Q: Why did the bus crash?

A: Because the driver was a loaf of bread.

Q: Why did the ship crash?

A: Because the captain was
a loaf of bread.

Q: Why did the bread van crash?

A: Accident investigators believe that it was due to a combination of factors, including high winds, icy roads, a dirty windshield, brake failure, four flat tires, and an indicator malfunction (plus the fact that the driver was a loaf of bread).

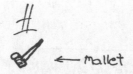

← mallet

Q: What has four legs; is big, green, and fuzzy; and would smush you if it fell out of a tree?

A: A pool table.

Q: **What's brown and sticky?**

A: A stick.

Q: What's orange and looks like an orange?

A: An orange.

snack food

It's the Story Police here. We've had reports of stupid jokes coming from this book, and you are our chief suspects.

Q: Why did the fly fall off the wall?

A: Because it had a piano tied to its leg.

Q: What's big and red
and eats rocks?

A: A big red rock-eater.

Q: What's big and red and
eats big red rock–eaters?

A: A big red big red rock-eater-
eater.

Q: Where does a general keep his armies?

A: Up his sleevies.

Q: Why did the refrigerator fall out of the tree?

A: Because it had no arms.

Q: What do you call a smart group of trees?

A: A brain forest.

Q: What did the rock say when it rolled into the tree?

A: Nothing—rocks don't talk.

Q: Which side of a tree has the most leaves?

A: The outside.

Q: How did Terry get hurt raking leaves?

A: He fell out of the tree.

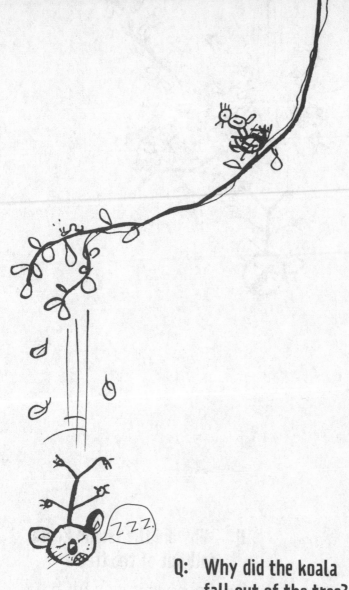

Q: Why did the koala
fall out of the tree?

A: Because it was asleep.

Q: Why did the second koala fall out of the tree?

A: Because it was hit by the first koala.

Q: **Why did the third koala fall out of the tree?**

A: Because it thought it was a game and joined in.

Q: **What did the worm say when its child came home late?**

A: "Where in earth have you been?"

Q: **What do you get if you cross a worm and a young goat?**

A: A dirty kid.

Q: How do you tell which end of
a worm is which?

A: Tickle it in the middle and
see which end laughs.

Q What's worse than
biting into an apple
and finding a worm?

A: Biting into an apple
and finding half a worm.

Q: Did you hear about the two silkworms that were in a race?

A: They ended up in a tie.

Q: What reads and lives in an apple?

A: A bookworm.

Andy Griffiths lives in an amazing treehouse with his friend Terry, and together they make funny books, just like the one you're holding in your hands right now. Andy writes the words, and Terry draws the pictures. If you'd like to know more, read the Treehouse series (or visit www.andygriffiths.com.au).

Terry Denton lives in an amazing treehouse with his friend Andy, and together they make funny books, just like the one you're holding in your hands right now. Terry draws the pictures, and Andy writes the words. If you'd like to know more, read the Treehouse series (or visit www.terrydenton.com).

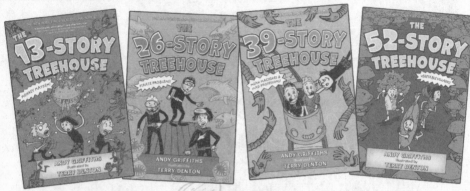